Unraveling Reading
The Basics of Learning to Read

By: Daniela Silva

Founder/Director of NHEG: Pamela S. Clark

Unraveling Reading
The Basics of Learning to Read

Founder/Director of NHEG: Pamela S. Clark
Author: Daniela Silva

Copyright © 2016
All rights reserved.
ISBN: 0692809376
ISBN-13: 978-0692809372 (New Heights Educational Group, Inc)
Library of Congress Control Number: 2016918991
New Heights Educational Group, Inc, Defiance, OHIO

DEDICATION

This book is dedicated in memory of Marli Silva dos Santos, my dear mother, first teacher and great enthusiast of my work.

And for my husband by the love deposited in me and in the development of this work.

CONTENTS

	Acknowledgments	i
1	Preface	1
2	New Heights Educational Group Mission	10
3	Introduction	11
4	Tutoring	13
5	Helping in Reading Acquisition	15
6	Skills in Grammar and Spelling	16
7	Activities to Improve Spelling and Writing Skills	18
8	The Influence and Benefits of Latin in English	20
9	The Use of Flashcards as a Didactic Teaching Resource	22
10	Dictionary Skills	25
11	Vocabulary Lists and How to Use Them	29
12	Reading Tips and Help	32
13	Developing the Writing: How to Develop This Practice in Children	36
14	Abbreviations: What They Are and How to Use Them	39
15	Using Calendar Words to Develop Capabilities in Reading and Writing	41
16	Working and Making Use of Contractions	44
17	Using Apostrophes in Holiday Words	48
18	Patience with Your Student: Understanding The Different Learning Styles of Children	51
19	Teaching Adult Students	58
20	Proposed Educational Strategies for Working with Students with Dyslexia and Reading Difficulties	66
21	Brain Gym Exercises	67
22	Conclusion	91
23	Dictionary	93

ACKNOWLEDGMENTS

New Heights Educational Group would like to recognize those who played a significant part in the creation of this book.

Foremost, to NHEG volunteer and author Daniela Silva, whose dream it was to write a book that would impact lives.

Pamela Clark spent many years exploring learning styles to help those who are hard to reach and their dedicated families. Her wish is for people to fall in love with learning and education and to never give up. NHEG further wishes to thank the author of the "Natural Speller" and creator of "Brain Gym" exercises for inspiring her and the families served by using their products.

Thank you to Ms. Clark's family (Greg, Mac and Lyndsey, Zach and Desiree) for their years of support and never giving up on the journey.

Thank you to the Spangler family (Cuyler, Kathryne, and Kailyn) for being our models for the exercises.

Special thanks to Shirley Li for the photos and the proofreaders/copy editors Rivan Stinson, Nibu Jacob, Faranak Aghdasi, Sheila Wright, Aditi Chopra and Jenni Schreiber, and formatting assistant, Jon Aitken.

Cover design by Pamela Clark, Marina Klimi and Ginnefine Jalloh.

PREFACE

New Heights Educational Group

New Heights Educational Group was created on June 1, 2006. Our initial goal was to offer help to all interested families regardless of school choice. We have grown by leaps and bounds since we were created. The mission for services was birthed from families coming together to better their lives and educational options. Over many years and during Founder/Director Pamela Clark's journey of discovery in bettering her children's education, Ms. Clark has explored many options including homeschooling, charter schools and local public school settings. Through her involvement with these educational systems, Ms. Clark has not only found strengths and weaknesses in these systems that affected her children's learning abilities, but she also encountered other families asking similar questions in order to improve their own children's educational experiences. In gathering these families together, Ms. Clark discovered that the families were able to help each other, especially in understanding how to teach children with learning difficulties such as ADHD, bipolar disorder, autism, neurological disorders and processing disorders. In addition to more successful, child-focused learning techniques, families further found themselves better able to cope with their children's struggles because of increased social support and shared skills. This experience gave credibility to Ms. Clark's vision of one day having a resource and literacy center that would function as a place for families to come for educational help and support.

We provide fill-in-the-gap type, one-on-one tutoring for youth and adults. All teachers and students are required to meet three hours a week over a three-day period. We found that fill-in-the gap type tutoring is necessary in reaching students that have been left behind in traditional settings. In addition, NHEG offers Enrichment Day classes locally to bring students together to learn themed based topics; this was not only to provide instruction but also to develop self-confidence, creativity, decision-making, leadership and public speaking skills. These enrichment classes provide opportunities where students - pre-K through high school – can learn something special. Many of these classes are led by students with teacher/tutor/volunteer supervision. This builds self-esteem in the students; as well, we've learned that students listen intently when another student is helping lead instructional classes.

During its operation, New Heights Educational Group has grown and has been able to clearly define a literacy program that is suited for all ages. It is the goal of the organization to continue to service all families in need; hence, we serve many new families a year. The organization also struggles in finding enough volunteers, staff and funding to help all those in need, especially for those who have limited income.

Pamela Clark

Ms. Clark, the founder and director of New Heights Educational Group, has 13 years of experience helping families with all their educational needs. With a passion for bettering education, she works tirelessly to improve the lives of families that come to her for assistance. She welcomes each family personally and helps them with whatever they need to further their goals. She also provides guidance to teachers and tutors, as well as monitors evaluations and provides training and resources to teachers and tutors for different learning styles. Her team of over 75 volunteers researches the latest advancements as well as uses past experience of what has worked to help new families.

Ms. Clark said, "My grandmother was the person that instilled a belief in me at a young age and a passion for bettering education and speaking up for what I believe in." Since then, the support of her husband and two sons as well as her co-founder and board member, Margaret Spangler, has played a vital role in the success of New Heights Educational Group. There have been many more who offered support to her and New Heights Educational Group, and even though all cannot be mentioned by name here, they are not forgotten.

Awards and Recognition

Defiance, Ohio – June 18, 2013 – Pamela S. Clark, founder and director of New Heights Educational Group, was presented with a Gold Stevie® Award in the category of *Executive of the Year—Nonprofit or Government Organizations* while New Heights Educational Group was presented with a Bronze Stevie® Award in the Category of *Company of the Year—Nonprofit or Government Organizations* in the 11th Annual American Business Awards in Chicago, Illinois. The American Business Awards is the nation's premier business awards program. All organizations operating in the U.S.A. are eligible to submit nominations—public and private, for-profit and nonprofit, large and small.

Awards won to date:

2016:

-- *Top-Rated Nonprofit* rating in GreatNonprofits

-- New Heights Educational Group was named *Organization of the Year – Non-Profit or Government, Silver - American Business Award*

2015:

-- *Top-Rated Nonprofit* rating in GreatNonprofits

--Pamela Clark (founder/executive director) received the *Bronze, Silver and Gold Presidential Volunteer Service Awards* and a letter from the White House signed by the President.

-- New Heights Educational Group was honored as Bronze Stevie® Award Winner: *American Business Awards*

-Founder/Executive Director Pamela Clark has been selected as a *Canyon Ranch Inspiration Award Winner.*

--Pamela Clark of New Heights Educational Group, named as Bronze Winner of the Stevie® Awards: *Sales & Customer Service*

--New Heights Educational Group was named 2nd place winner for the TechSoup.org *Remote Work Success Story Campaign!*

2014:

--*Top-Rated Nonprofit* rating in GreatNonprofits

--Bronze Stevie® American Business Award: *Executive of the Year for Nonprofit or Government Organization*

--*Certificate of Recognition of Achievement* from Sherrod Brown, United States Senate

--*Certificate of Recognition of Achievement* from Keith Faber, Ohio Senate

--*Certificate of Recognition of Achievement* from Governor and Lieutenant Governor of Ohio

2013:

--Ohio Secretary of State Jon Husted listed New Heights Educational Group in *Great Ohio-Based Nonprofit Organizations*

--*Gold Participant* rating in GuideStar Exchange

--*Top-Rated Nonprofit* rating in GreatNonprofits

--Silver Stevie® Women in Business Award: *Organization of the Year Government or Nonprofit with 10 or Less Employees*

--Silver International Business Award: *Company of the Year Government or Non-Profit Organization*

--Bronze American Business Award: *Company of the Year Nonprofit or Government Organization*

--Gold Stevie® American Business Award: *Executive of the Year for Government or Nonprofit Organization*

--Bronze Stevie® Women in Business Award: *Executive of the Year for Founder/Director of a Government or Nonprofit with 10 or Less Employees*

2012:

>--Silver Stevie® Women in Business Award: *Organization of the Year Government or Nonprofit Organization*

>--Bronze Stevie® Women in Business Award: *Female Innovator of the Year in a Government or Nonprofit Organization with 10 or Less Employees*

To read letters sent to New Heights Educational Group, please visit:
http://www.newheightseducation.org/who-we-are/letters-of-support/

For media and press, please visit:

http://www.newheightseducation.org/who-we-are/nheg-press/

Daniela Silva

Daniela Silva is from Brazil and holds a degree in Pedagogy with concentrations in School Management and Business Education. She also has a postgraduate degree in Personnel Management and Neuroeducation. Working with e-Learning and personnel development social projects since 2009, Mrs. Silva is motivated to transform lives through knowledge. She also writes web columns about education, covering the following topics: teaching practices in the classroom; emotions and learning; evaluation and school planning learning disorders; homeschooling; brain child development; and education and personnel training. As a manager of educational media for a school support project, her responsibilities included analyzing and selecting quality content for both student and teacher academic training. Additionally, she develops courses and training manuals for teachers and students and contributes as a mentor to an online platform, answering questions about career plans, college decisions, personal development and professional skills.

Since 2012, Ms. Silva has contributed voluntarily as an educational writer for New Heights Educational Group, as well as develops and researches material on education for websites, magazines and teaching materials. The articles and materials developed include content for educational assistance to families, school orientation activities, curriculum and programs, youth and adult education, as well as technical and pedagogical practices.

The following articles written by Daniela Silva can be found here on NHEG's website: http://www.newheightseducation.org/who-we-are/nheg-press/nheg-articles/

- *Developing The Potential in Children With Attention Deficit Disorder Hyperactivity*
- *Autism Spectrum Disorder*
- *Homeschool Curriculum*
- *A New Perspective Of Educating*
- *Online Tutoring for Your Child.Html*
- *Educational Technology In The Development Of Adult*
- *The Distance Education Option*
- *Volunteer Education*
- *Adult Learning*

DanielaS_Writer@NewHeightsEducation.org

NEW HEIGHTS EDUCATIONAL GROUP MISSION

New Heights Educational Group, Inc. promotes literacy for children and adults by offering a range of educational support services. Such services include: assisting families in the selection of schools; organization of educational activities; and acquisition of materials. We promote a healthy learning environment and enrichment programs for families of preschool and school-age children, including children with special needs.

3 INTRODUCTION

Learning to read is very different from learning to speak. To learn to read well, children need to know the sounds of the letters and the meanings of the words. However, even if the child does not understand the meaning of a word, the student may be able to identify some letters in other sentences through their visual characteristics. From there, the student begins to realize that the words produce sounds, constituting phonemes, and by associating these sounds with written words, the child is able to read a sentence.

However, when it comes to adult education, the apprenticeship occurs differently from a child's learning. The adult values education practices involving knowledge and experiences accumulated throughout life. Thus, when teaching an adult student, it is necessary that the teacher consider all cultural adult experiences, so that the student may be able to use and apply the educational content in a practical way when solving problems in his or her day-to-day life.

For children with language-based learning disabilities, there is difficulty in understanding, memorizing, and learning some information and knowledge, and this occurs because the brain collects and processes the information in a way that affects the comprehension and the development of learning. The good news is that, currently, there are new techniques and pedagogical strategies based on movement that can help these students with difficulties improve performance in writing and reading by developing focus, concentration, and attention in academic activities. It is about the Brain Gym, a pedagogical approach that combines the mind and body with movements that incorporate learning in a ludic and dynamic way.

Unraveling Reading is the first book in a series of books being published by New Heights Educational Group (NHEG), a national and international award-winning educational nonprofit organization located in Ohio. This first book is written by Daniela Silva, from Brazil, who volunteers her time and has spent a number of years writing this book.

The book is meant to be a guide for those who are looking for assistance and guidance when trying to reach a student of any age that needs to learn to read and improve vocabulary and spelling skills. NHEG has used these methods to teach many so-called hard-to-reach students, including those with developmental issues and with special needs. The aim of this book is to show that anyone of any age can learn to read. In addition, it aims to unravel any frustration previously felt and replace that with feelings of achievement when learning to read.

4 TUTORING

Reading Tips and Help

1. Take a week to go over teachers' manuals and learn about how to teach with Laubach's Effective Adult Learning System. You can find these books either at the NHEG library, by visiting your local library, or by purchasing them online.

   http://proliteracyednet.org/articles.asp?mcid=2&rid=564

   Notes:

   1. This can sometimes be used for teens, depending on the situation.

   2. You do not have to follow each suggestion to the letter.

   3. Determine if the student sees better with more or less white space on the page. Pamela Clark suggests having the student screened for Irlen Syndrome. Visit this website (http://irlen.com/), or if you are local to NHEG, Pamela Clark can provide screening.

The Spelling Side

1. Use Natural Speller by Kathryn Stout for teaching spelling. Each week the student will have a spelling and vocabulary list.

2. Each week, you teach a sound or pattern. Do one sound or pattern at a time, and never give more than 30 words.

Vocabulary

1. Every word that the student misses when reading should become a vocabulary word.

2. The student needs to study these with you every time you meet.

Practice vocabulary after the reading exercise and before the end of the day. You can also write the words on a flip chart for practice.

5 HELPING IN READING ACQUISITION: TIPS FOR ENCOURAGING CHILDREN TO READ

Prior to encouraging the child to practice reading, it is necessary to awaken motivation and curiosity using some literature that interests the student. Invite the child to go with you to a bookstore or library, and offer them the opportunity to choose books that both of you can read together. The ideal type of literature for your child is one that is appropriate for your child's age and cognitive development.

Respect the duration the child can handle. Mark the last page read and continue the next day.

6 SKILLS IN GRAMMAR AND SPELLING

The ability to spell is developed from the knowledge that the child has of word structure. The orthographic (or visual) memory and the perception that children have of the word sounds are used in this process. Furthermore, the ability to identify and point out similarities between words also helps to stimulate the child's grammar skills. This means that, while the child may not understand the meaning of a word, he or she may be able to identify its letters in other sentences through its visual characteristics.

After identifying similar letters in other words, the child realizes that these letters produce speech sounds making it possible to associate the letter with its phoneme, thus acquiring an understanding between the letter and the sound that comes out of it when it is spoken. In an initial stage, it is common for children to spell according to phonetic spelling, for example: bed (bad); sad (said), buk (book); kam (came); lov (love). To the extent that this stage advances and the child acquires greater orthographic conscience, meaning the student is able to elaborate new words from pieces of letters they already know, such as "actor" and "actress", "cook" and "cooker", "pen" and "pencil", "life" and "like".

To acquire the skill of writing, it is necessary that the child understand the combination of letters, the rules that compose them and their phonic elements. To the extent that the student develops reading and writing skills, the child realizes that most sounds are the result of combinations of letters. In this step, it is common for children to get confused in the spelling of some words, such as "white" and "walking."

When the student advances in his/her development of spelling, the student is able to understand not only how to spell each word but also its graphic significance.

The learning and the cognitive storing of new words and meanings encourages the student to spell before writing. Through practical examples, associations between words written in a similar way, and through analogies, the child acquires the ability to spell more easily, such as in the words "house" and "mouse."

The academic skills in spelling are achieved when the child is able to understand the structure that composes the words, their sounds and syllables.

In practicing in the classroom, the teacher can group lists of words having the same grammatical pattern. The student will be able to remember a word through the association of a similar word.

A ludic way to teach spelling is to use the senses so that the child sees the word they are learning: feeling the contour with a finger over the letters that compose it; saying and repeating the corresponding sounds of the word; and spelling its syllables. In spelling, it is possible to make a game to play with the child by showing the student the introduction of prefixes and suffixes in a word. For example, adding "un" to "happy," to become a new word "unhappy."

Practice precedes excellence, so it is necessary to provide the child time for practice exercises and activities where the student has the opportunity to listen to a word, put it in context and then reflect on how to write it and what it means.

7 ACTIVITIES TO IMPROVE SPELLING AND WRITING SKILLS

1. Family groups of words

Choose a group of words that the child is familiar with (toys, names of family members, candy, etc.). Bring the student word strips (which can be typed or written in large letters form) containing the same phoneme, such as ball, doll, etc.

Ask students to read them aloud, making them notice the similarities between the same ending sounds. Thus, the child can make connections between words, being able to remember the word from their memory of other similar words.

2. Working with the movable alphabet

If the child is successful with the words used in the process described above, use mobile alphabet letters to write the words and have the child read each word with you in a loud voice. After this, separate the syllables and then observe the child, focusing on the pronunciation of every syllable, making the student swipe a finger on the letters of each word.

3. Hunting words, prefixes and suffixes

Present to the child three boxes, each containing prefixes, suffixes, and word patterns. Present to the child a small box containing several words. Ask the child to remove from within this box a word. With this word in hand, the child (with help) will have to write on the blackboard the suffix and the prefix belonging to this word. This activity can be repeated daily for 30 minutes.

4. Meaning of the words

Using a dictionary, help the child search for the meanings of words worked in activities 1 and 2. Question the student on how each word can be applied in everyday life and if he or she has already seen these words in another place.

5. Answer quiz questions

Give the student a quiz based on each word studied. Draw an item from a bag containing word patterns, suffixes, or prefixes. Show the child the word, asking:

The word I have in my hand: is it a prefix, a suffix, or a word pattern?
The word is modified when you add a suffix or prefix. How?
How are the sounds in this word pronounced? How are the syllables separated?

6. Reading a story

Read a story to the child. After this, ask the student if there are some words of which he or she doesn't know the meaning. Read, in the dictionary, the meaning of these words and write them out, separating the word pattern, prefix and suffix. Then cover parts of the word with a colorful card, and ask, *What is the part of the word that I'm showing: prefix, suffix, or word pattern?*

8 THE INFLUENCE AND BENEFITS OF LATIN IN ENGLISH

The English language originated from Anglo-Frisian dialects of Germanic invaders, but some words have a great influence of Latin sources. Some examples of Germanic words with a Latin origin are *butter, cheese, dish, egg yolk, and kitchen*. In addition, groups of Christians who were on a mission in Great Britain brought with them a language with words derived from Latin such as *apostle, minister, monk, nun, priest, and school*.

The Latin language and the English language are similar because they are a part of the same family, Indo-European. However, it is possible to observe some contrasts between the two languages. In English, an article must accompany the noun characterizing it (*a* house, *an* anchor); however, in Latin, it is not necessary to use nouns with articles.

The study of the Latin language has a number of benefits for the young student:

1. Organization of thoughts: Latin is a language that requires organization and attention to development of thoughts and speaking. These skills are important not only for the improvement and study of a language but also in learning content in science and mathematics.

2. Improvement in language development: Children who choose to study Latin in school will find it easier to develop language and grammar in English because the spelling and vocabulary of the English language has roots in Latin.

3. Greater skill to learn other languages: Learning from Latin prepares the child to develop skills in other languages more easily. This occurs when the student has some previous experience in oral and grammatical construction of words.

4. Preparation to deal with diversity: Learning about the origin of words and the construction of sentences can teach students that, in our society, there are different people with different cultures and ways of life, but they may also have similarities with people of other origins.

As noted, Latin, when aligned with the school curriculum and with a pedagogical proposal, can develop academic and social skills essential for personal development, and aid in the acquisition of new languages, as well as teaching new cultures.

9 THE USE OF FLASHCARDS AS A DIDACTIC TEACHING RESOURCE

Flashcards are cards that group a set of questions and answers, which can be applied in school to subjects such as math, English, history, geography, or any subject that requires the student's reading and comprehension of questions and answers. The operation of this feature works as follows:

1. The student removes a card from the pile and reads it.

2. After reading the question, the student attempts to answer.

3. If answered correctly, the card is moved to a separate pile of cards to which the student knows the answer to the question.

4. If the student does not know the answer, the card is moved to the block of cards to be reviewed again later.

Flashcards adopt the system of spaced repetition, which is reviewing information (contained in the cards as questions and answers) at intervals of increasing time. On the computer, this system is programmed at intervals to meet the demands of student learning. Teacher tools to create and implement your own flashcard application to be used in virtual classes can be found online.

Psychologist Howard Gardner authored the book *Frames of Mind: The Theory of Multiple Intelligences* that features seven types of intelligences present in humans: logical-mathematical, linguistic, bodily-kinesthetic, musical, pictorial, interpersonal, and intrapersonal. Each of these intelligences focuses on a function or ability.

For Gardner, each individual has his/her own characteristics and interests, as well as intelligence or academic ability. Thus, the teacher must see each student as a unique being, with his/her own way of learning and developing.

Visual intelligence is the most prevalent among students. The teacher can prepare and develop activities using this type of intelligence to complement the learning of the student A good example of a pedagogical activity that encourages the visual capabilities of the student is flashcards, especially ones that present a fun and colorful feature and get the child's attention.

To the extent that students become familiar with the use and learning of flashcards in the classroom, the same resource can be suggested and implemented at home by parents and children.

The flashcards can be acquired through printed textbooks or e-books; they can also be handmade and illustrated using pictures from magazines, drawings, or computer resources. It is important that all cards are the same size with different colors for each type of activity.

In the classroom, the teacher can ask each group of students to build a set of flashcards with a specific theme. Producing their own flashcards, besides being more economical, provides a greater sense of empowerment and motivation for students because they, themselves, are responsible for making the material used for their education.

Examples of educational activities using the flashcards as a resource:

1. Memory game: Students, sitting in circles, must memorize and name the most pairs (drawings or figures) contained in the cards.

2. Identifying the meaning of words: On one side of the card, the teacher can put a word in a different language (e.g., Spanish, English, or Latin). The child, seeing the word written on the card,

tries to define the word's meaning, which is written on the other side of the card.

3. Mental calculation: At the edge of the card, the student will have a math problem, which may be an addition, subtraction, multiplication, or division problem. The answer will be at the bottom of the card but covered with a piece of colored paper; the student will have to answer this math problem. The purpose of this activity is to set and perform the greatest number of calculations described on the card, mentally and in an agile way.

10 DICTIONARY SKILLS

Why Are They So Important? How Are They Developed in Children?

Skillful use of a dictionary is an important ability for academic development and practical life skills. Dictionary skills include the ability to: 1) alphabetize by the first and second letters of a word; 2) count syllables in a word as they are spoken or use phonetic pronunciation to indicate each syllable; 3) know and understand the rules of syllabic division, which can be found in Natural Speller, by Kathryn Stout; 4) recognize root words, prefixes and suffixes; and 5) know and understand the rules of combining words into compound words.

The desire to know words and their meanings helps the reader to better understand text and context, which is the knowledge and interpretation of both what is read and what is experienced. In practice, the more a learner has access to information and communication, the greater the chances of this child or adult learning and expanding her or his vocabulary and spelling repertoire.

It is the educator's role, when attempting to increase a reader's vocabulary, to stimulate curiosity and motivation in that student to discover new words and new ways of expressing his or her cultural repertoire.

In the course of educational practice, the teacher can encourage students' desires to learn the meaning of new words by asking them to read a text/story and underline words that they don't yet know, then assist the learner in locating the meaning of each word in a dictionary.

The life experiences of the student can also help in the learning of new words and sentences. This occurs, for example, when a child observes his or her parents:

- reading a magazine or newspaper and asking about what they are reading;
- readily reading or telling stories to them;
- willingly agreeing to spell a certain word (such as someone's name or part of an address);
- showing interest in the child's world by talking often with them about his or her day or what he or she learned in school.

The student's learning level is a factor in what dictionary skills should be taught. The teacher/tutor/parent needs to understand what should be taught and when it should be taught. We believe these should be taught at the correct time for the best learning implementation.

Examples

Third grade skills that should be built upon range from alphabetizing by first, second, and third letters in a word, guiding students to turn to different sections of a dictionary and looking up words in those sections, identifying guide words and entry words, and pointing those out to students, matching words to their dictionary respellings, dividing words into syllables and marking accented syllables, identifying many antonyms and synonyms at different learning levels, using pronunciation keys and teaching words that have more than one meaning.

Fourth grade skills that should be built upon range from alphabetizing by first, second, third and fourth letters in a word as well as continuing the third grade level activities using the fourth grade list of spelling words being taught.

Fifth grade skills that should be built upon range from alphabetizing through the fifth letter continuing from fourth grade level, reading and writing phonetic respellings, identifying various meanings for a word, using pronunciation keys, writing words in syllables and marking each accented syllable, and teaching the etymology of each word.

Sixth grade skills should focus on alphabetizing through any letter, identifying and using entry and guide words, reading and using phonetic respellings, identifying various meanings for a word, using a dictionary's pronunciation keys, identifying antonyms and synonyms, writing words in syllables and marking all accented syllables, identifying the parts of speech to which a word belongs by using a dictionary and continuing skills learned.

You continue teaching these methods for all learning levels.

Encourage the child to make a habit of reading. Reading increases vocabulary, improves verbal fluency and provides spelling practice. Books contain a vast and rich world of words so they can expand the cultural universe of the student, instill the curiosity and promote the learning of new words.

In the classroom, teachers can propose activities that encourage dialogue and debate, using texts and topics of interest to the child as a didactic resource, calling attention to the meaning of each new word in different contexts.

The words will have meaning and significance to the learner to the extent that the student can find the same word in different contexts, as many times as possible. Students can practice dictionary skills when encountering a new word or find a word already known in a different context.

An interesting tip when working on vocabulary in the classroom can be to assemble a panel containing the new words learned by students in reading, grammar or spelling activities. They can write the words in the panel. In another activity, each student can choose a word and give clues for classmates to guess its meaning.

The teacher can also encourage the class to develop a collective dictionary, containing the new words the students learned during the semester. The teacher can even rally the class for a "game of words" where the teacher would say a sentence containing the meaning of a word and the students would mark the word's name by placing a bean on a card with the correct answer.

At home, parents can develop the habit of using a dictionary with the aim of helping the child to search the meaning of a word, either while doing homework or during family reading. Another way to work with the dictionary at home or in the classroom is to instruct the child to form sentences with the new words that they learned that day or week.

Depending on number of words given to student these sentences should be divided up over two days.

11 VOCABULARY LISTS AND HOW TO USE THEM

In order to understand what is being read, the meaning of the sentences must be clear. Besides reading out loud and searching for the meaning of words in the dictionary, it is necessary for the reader to associate the new words with simple situations in everyday life. For example, in the sentence:

"The student waited for the opportune moment to speak with the teacher about his grade."

The educator may ask the student about the meaning of the word "opportune" in this context.

- What does the author mean by "opportune moment?" Why does the student decide to wait to talk to the teacher instead of speaking about it during class?
- Is there anyone here who has ever heard the word "opportune" in any other situation? What was the situation?
- In what other phrases can we use the word "opportune?" Give some examples.

Books and literature that give definitions of phrases and words with their context (and history of use) may help the reader to learn different uses and meanings of the word. It is important that the educator pauses while reading to explain the words and expressions mentioned in the text.

Before giving any definition of the word, it is necessary that the teacher makes the student understand the word by encouraging the student to think and reflect on the possible definition of the word.

Learning needs to be endowed with meaning and value to the reader in a way that the reader can learn words that are part of daily life—either at home, on trips, at the zoo, on vacation with family or even when they are watching television. In this way, the reader can associate the word with something in everyday life. Such associations will help the child memorize the word easily.

To develop vocabulary in very young children, the teacher can work with the students to construct sentences based on their experiences, worldview, stories, etc. This will help comprehension and solidify sense and meaning. Concrete examples of experiences and the personal connection help children with the construction of names and to learn the significance of the objects.

For practice in the classroom, the following activities can assist in building and developing students' vocabularies:

1. Develop sentences using the words:
   - Develop a sentence using words with opposite meaning, or *antonyms*.
   - Develop a sentence using words with similar meaning, or *synonyms*.

2. Perform a dictation to the class:
   Then, with the help of a dictionary, ask each student to correct the words he or she wrote down.

3. Memory game for synonyms:
   Propose a memory game using synonyms. Cards are distributed to a group of students. Students turn over one card, then try to find the card with the similar word on it (*house* and *home*, for example).

A match will be successful if the two cards flipped over are synonyms. If the two cards flipped over are not synonyms, they must be returned to their original spot, face down, for another try.

4. Hunting words:

    Write a group of adjectives on the blackboard. Using a mobile alphabet, the students have to write the antonym of each word.

12 READING TIPS AND HELP

The exercise described below will help further improve the student's reading skill.

1. Let the student pick a book.

2. Explain to the student that they need to sit right next to you while reading and that you will write the words down that are missed. Tell the student not to get upset about it and to only pay attention to reading and not to you. (There should be no physical touching.)

3. Write down all the words that the student misses. If the list is not written neatly, type the list on the computer. All letters/words need to be easily seen by the student. You might want to print the list daily in case your computer fails.

4. Do not interrupt the student when they are reading. Stop after each page, and tell the student the words that were missed. Point out each word in the book and on your notes.

5. After they read two or three pages for 15 minutes (or whatever you feel is right), place a bookmark in the book for the next day.

6. Ask the student for two of their favorite colors. Tell them that you are using the colors to mark the words to show their progress. Put all the words they can sound out in one color, and once they learn them well, you will put them in the other color, resulting in two colored columns. After they remember them for a week to two weeks, take them off the list.

7. Go over words they missed. Give the student one or two chances to recognize the word, and then tell them what it is. Do this with all words.

8. The student, with a partner (such as a spouse, a friend, or a parent), needs to go over vocabulary words every single day. The student can take at least one day off on the weekend.

9. Tell the student to read something every day. Use erasable highlighters if necessary. Each word that the student misses when reading becomes a vocabulary word. This can be assigned as homework for the student to study at home.

10. Do not let the student give up! The student will need to continue with this all school year—maybe even for longer than the one year. The more the student practices and the longer they stick with it, the more they will learn and the better they will read. Do this after the reading exercise of the chapter 12 (Reading Tips and Help), and before the end of the day. A flip chart can also be used.

Keep notes/records on the student's progress, problem areas and improvements from the first day to the last.

Spelling Pretest

1. Do not let the student see the list of new spelling words before the pretest. Say each word and have the student write it the way they think it is spelled. After they complete the pretest, grade it, and tell them that they did a great job, even if the student misses a lot of the pretest words. This task should be fun and never a punishment or chore. You are using it as a tool to better them. Write the correct word next to the missed words to study as homework.

2. Monday: Ask the student if they know the meanings of his or her words. If they say "yes," quiz them. You will find that many do not know all the meanings of the words. Make sure that they know how to look up words in a dictionary. If they have assistance at home, it would be a great homework assignment. Work on this before starting sentences. Have the student write or verbally give sentences for assigned words. If many words are missed, divide the words (Note: This is also important for students with poor handwriting skills or with special needs.)

3. Tuesday: Have the student write or verbally give sentences for the remaining assigned words.

4. Homework: Have the student practice writing their missed words and tell them to study the words. (Writing of the words can be done on a chalk or dry erase board. You can take a picture of the boards for reference.)

5. Wednesday: A fun crossword puzzle or other fun game for the spelling words could be shared on this day. Many special needs students do not like crossword puzzles; find something they like, and stick with it. Remember learning is supposed to be fun.

6. Thursday: Give the student a spelling bee—this can be done verbally or on paper. You will have the student's original pretest to work from and mark "OK" if they learned the word. (You do want to see the student's homework. Make sure you check it.) Remember to praise them for any words they get correct, and tell them they only need to study missed words for Friday's test.

7. Friday: Give a spelling test with all words that were missed on Thursday's test, and give a pretest for the next sound pattern. Any words that the student missed on Thursday need to be on Friday's test. If the student still misses them, add those words to the following week's sound/pattern. If there are a lot of missed words, you will need to start again on Monday with the same word set containing only the missed words from Friday's test.

8. When teaching spelling words, watch for reversals of letters (some reversals are normal) on a regular basis, and ask the student if he or she has problems seeing the words. Do they look blurry? Do the words move? If the student says "yes," contact NHEG or some other educational professional. The flip chart can also be used.

13 DEVELOPING WRITING: HOW TO HELP THIS PRACTICE IN CHILDREN

The practice of writing can be introduced gradually in the child's life, in a pleasant and enjoyable way, without seeming tiresome or boring. The child may show greater interest in developing written materials or content from subjects that have some meaning or spark curiosity in him or her, such as imitating the grammatical style of a favorite author or developing a topic or theme that captures their attention.

Children are interested in activities that have a social function in their lives, for example, writing an email to a distant friend or a posting to a blog, developing a different ending to a story, planning a poem and writing it, creating dialogues or subtitles for photos or prints.

A ludic way to stimulate your child to write can be to introduce classroom activities in which they can write and describe the personal characteristics of people in their family, such as parents, uncles and grandparents. Children can use a photo they bring with them and write about it—where the photo was taken, who was there that day or why this picture was chosen.

The practice leads to excellence. This way one learns to write by writing. The teacher can suggest attractive themes for the child in which to develop sentences, paragraphs and texts. The child's work may be revised by the teacher, who can also suggest tips to improve the written content, complimenting each advancement the student makes in his or her work.

Stimulate the child's creative thinking to help them prepare essays and compositions, as well as practice analysis and interpretation to reflect on what they've read and how to write about it later; this can be a very productive way to encourage the student's motivation for reading and writing. Through these practices, you will not only be developing readers and writers but also individuals able to argue and form opinions.

You can also instill in students the habit of reading and looking up words for which they don't know the meaning in the dictionary. Thus, in addition to learning the meaning of new words, students can also widen their linguistic repertoire, taking notice of the synonyms contained in the dictionary.

The narrative is a pedagogical practice that contributes positively to the development of writing and to the enrichment of the child's vocabulary. When a story is told (and developed in written form), the child needs to list the facts in an orderly manner, while the sentences are constructed and arranged in the form of new vocabulary. You can encourage this practice in the classroom, suggesting topics for writing that are part of the story of a child's life, such as a trip with the family, a short trip during the holidays, an event with friends, etc. In this way, the students will learn to develop a written narrative in a clear, organized, and succinct manner, while exercising the capacities of argumentation, creativity, and explanation of ideas.

The goal is to awaken the child's motivation for writing. Suggest activities with themes of interest to the student, such as composing papers on favorite books or movies, writing letters, invitations, or emails to anyone. It is important that you orient students to writing the texts, taking into consideration their strengths and capabilities, without requiring a lot of the student at this early stage of the compositions.

During the development of the activity, you can lead the children to reflect on their own written work, instead of simply criticizing them by pointing out their mistakes, especially with the red pen, for example. Regarding the orientation of writing, it's important to review the work, teaching the children about punctuation, spelling, textual coherence and cohesion. Guide the students in relation to the chronological order of textual production—with an introduction, development and conclusion of ideas. Furthermore, it is essential that the children have in their minds who will be the target audience of their writing, as well as the types of pronouns, verbs, and adjectives that will be part of their text.

14 ABBREVIATIONS: WHAT THEY ARE AND HOW TO USE THEM

Abbreviations are shortened words used to refer to certain topics or subjects, thus representing expressions in a reduced form. They have to be used judiciously in order not to compromise the meaning of the words. It is the representation of a word using symbols or letters, generally applied to give a different intonation to the word.

In practice, an abbreviation is written by omitting certain letters or syllables, as, for example, in the word *Professor* written as *Prof.* in texts and scientific articles. Abbreviations are often used to show names and terms, adding more fluidity and understanding to the content. Some common examples where abbreviations are used are in professional academic titles, names of streets or avenues, names of companies and institutions, professional jargon and in current electronic communication.

The growing number of abbreviations in written communication reflects the speed and immediacy of communication in the present day and the increasing changes in the world and in society—as in the case of the new technology used on the Internet such as blogs, Twitter, and Facebook.

Learning abbreviations can make the text easier to read. Many people, when faced with some abbreviations in an article, can remember the meaning of terms and longer words through association between them and the abbreviation.

In a practical way, the student can take note of abbreviations already understood and separate them by sections or themes, such as names of streets, academic titles, days of the week, months of the year, etc.

As a pedagogical activity applied as a final project, you might suggest the class develop murals or panels with the abbreviations they studied, or create a book containing the respective abbreviations. In addition, students can participate in a memory game through the use of colored cards; the child that draws a card containing the abbreviation *Dr.* will have to find the other card containing the word *Doctor*. Another suggestion is writing a dictionary containing words and abbreviations for the bibliographic archive of the school. The most important thing is that the activity is fun and attractive, and at the same time, the child feels motivated to learn.

15 USING CALENDAR WORDS TO DEVELOP CAPABILITIES IN READING AND WRITING

The calendar, in addition to guiding educators and tutors in planning activities and routine tasks, can also be used as a teaching tool in the development of some academic competencies. First, the calendar, as an element of organization and time management, can stimulate students in the orientation of their tasks' deadlines. For example, encouraging students to use a colored pen to mark the calendar the days corresponding with each activity that will be evaluated by the tutor will teach them values such as organization, responsibility and discipline—important characteristics for commitment to any academic activity.

Here are some suggested activities educators can use to develop competencies that involve reading and writing words:

- Work with words that refer to the calendar. You can bring the students a calendar with blank spaces on each day of the week. Students can use the blank spaces to record the theme of the class activities performed on that day. For example, they can note on the calendar what themed tasks were completed on that day, such as nouns, phonemes, among others. In this way, everyone can orally pronounce the written theme word with the teacher, verifying with her the correct way to write it.

- Suggest that the student write a personal calendar, with the months and days of the week and the content that is to be learned. Ask the child to color every Monday with a specific color and to write the subject of this day (for example, mathematics, English, and so on, with all the other days filled with different colors). This activity develops skills in spelling and the notion of time and space.

- Work with the child on the notion of sequence and order. Create strips of paper with the name of each day of the week. Present the child with the strips shuffled. Encourage them to put the days of the week in the correct sequence, placing them side-by-side (later this activity can be repeated using the months of the year).

- Encourage the child to create a diary in the form of a calendar where the student has the opportunity to develop small paragraphs on extra class activities that can be conducted with the family. For the introduction of each month, the child can select and attach a picture that illustrates the meaning of the main activities in that month. Writing skills and spatial skills are developed in this task.

- At the beginning of each class, develop with the students the routine of the day, writing the day's activities on a calendar made with white cardboard hung on the class wall. In this way, children develop concepts such as autonomy and organization of time and tasks as well as expand vocabulary by the writing of new words on the calendar.

- At the end of each month, talk to the child about your impressions of the completed month and encourage the student to write about the events or lessons he or she enjoyed the most during this month. In this activity, oral and written language skills are exercised.

- Create a dictionary calendar where each day you can explain the meaning of a new word to the class. These words may be related to the reading of a book during the class, a discussion with the students on a particular topic, or even a question or curiosity brought by a child from home.

It is important that the activities developed instigate curiosity and the child's motivation for learning. For this reason, the planning of ludic contents that are age-appropriate as well as developmentally appropriate is fundamental to the students' acquisition of knowledge and learning. Using a word calendar to teach subjects offers the teacher and student a world of possibilities to be explored.

16 WORKING AND MAKING USE OF CONTRACTIONS

Contractions are the shortest form of a word. It occurs when there are two words, and this is transformed into one word, such as in *you are* being transformed to *you're*.

Contractions are part of oral and written language, widely used in daily communication by people and in the transmission of a message, as in the following excerpt:

- From *Do not go there* to *Don't go there*

In order to change the spelling of two words, turning them into a unit, an apostrophe is used, as in the examples below:

- You are: you're
- I will: I'll
- They will: they'll
- Will not: won't
- Did not: didn't
- You would: you'd
- What will: what'll
- Should not: shouldn't
- Must not: mustn't

Grammatically, the use of contractions is not required in creating a text; however, usage in written language creates texts that are more accessible and in colloquial for the reader, causing the feeling of closeness to the message. In the development of content for advertising, or in works in which space limitation or restriction of characters is required, the use of contractions is essential. On the other hand, using contractions in papers or in formal conversations, as in academic research or business letters, may not be recommended.

Teaching contractions in a practical way

Explain to the child that the apostrophe is a punctuation mark used to make shorter words. In practice, the apostrophe is used to take the place of the omitted letters, as in the case of the word *I've*, where the apostrophe takes the place of the letters *ha* (I *ha*ve).

Among examples of activities for teaching contractions are:

- **Hunting words**

    Using a small verse of a text, the child must circle the words that contain an apostrophe.

- **Transcribe the phrase**

    The child must rewrite the sentences using the corresponding contraction for each word.

- **Reply card**

    Shuffle some cards and place them on the table. The child turns over a card with the word *I am* for example. Then the student needs to turn over another card and check if it contains the answer with the corresponding apostrophe, in this case, *I'm*.

- **Word transformed**

    Distribute to children strips of paper containing words written with an apostrophe. Each child should write on the other side of the strip of paper: the word as a contraction or the word written without the use of the apostrophe. At the end of the activity, ask each student to write their words on the flip chart.

- **Making a composition**

   Suggest contractions to the student and have them prepare and essay making use of them.

- **Sentence attached**

   Bring to class strips of cardboard (that are attached with adhesive tape to the wall) containing two words, for example, *they will*. The child must find the card containing the contraction—in this case *they'll*—and attach it to the wall next to the corresponding word.

- **Exchange of emails**

   This activity can be done at two different times in the classroom. One week, ask the children to write emails to school friends using informal language, making use of contractions in the writing. In another week, print the emails the students have written and ask them to rewrite them using formal language without the use of contractions in the content.

17 USING APOSTROPHES IN HOLIDAY WORDS

Working with activities emphasizing the use of apostrophes in holiday words can be a ludic and attractive way to teach spelling to children. The teacher can make use of annual holidays by integrating them into lessons and activities, valuing the meaning and the experience that these dates have for students, transforming them into relevant educational issues in the classroom.

In practice, the use of the apostrophe is applied in the following cases:

Holiday words with an apostrophe before the *s*:
- New Year's Day
- Valentine's Day
- Saint Patrick's Day

Holiday words with an apostrophe after the *s*:
- Presidents' Day
- Mothers' Day

And holiday words with no apostrophe:
- United Nations Day
- Rosa Parks Day

Examples of fun activities using holiday themes:

- Introduce the child to messages in cards, letters, or emails containing the writing of holiday themes, and ask if this student has ever observed this written in some other text or content. From this, you can establish a dialogue with the child about the written word, reading it aloud, trying to identify the letters that compose the sentence.

- Write holiday words using different textured paper, colors and shapes, with the objective being to know and become familiar with the full written word.

- Words and wordplay: Take from inside a small bag a themed holiday word and then ask the child to write words in print form and then in cursive.

- Creative writing: Have the student write a card (for someone special), using any of the holiday themes discussed in class. In this activity, the child will have the opportunity to improve his or her spelling and develop his or her creativity.

- Thematic calendar: Create along with the child a thematic calendar using the holiday themes for each corresponding month, encouraging the child to write the name of each holiday. The text can also be further developed in this activity by writing the historical significance of each holiday in your calendar.

- Unscramble the word: Using a mobile alphabet, the teacher can present to the child the word of a holiday, "New Year's Day" for example, in a scrambled way so the student can put it in the correct order.

18 PATIENCE WITH YOUR STUDENT: UNDERSTANDING THE DIFFERENT LEARNING STYLES OF CHILDREN

Patience when teaching is crucial in so many ways; significant damage can be done to a student's self-esteem and willingness to learn if care isn't taken. In the opinion of Pamela Clark, founder of NHEG, you must remove yourself from the equation. If you aren't reaching the student by previous attempts, she says, "you need to adapt to the student, casting all ideas of what you personally think is the right way to learn. Only then will you see a breakthrough."

Learning is a process that involves different techniques and practices. For the development of new skills and abilities, the human brain uses different stimuli and ways to capture the information. Thus, the act of learning includes practicing diverse forms of apprenticeship that are independent of a unique method or learning style.

Each child is different from another child; presenting your own way to processing the knowledge defines your particular style of apprenticeship. There is no good or bad teaching method; what exists are different ways to conceive the information, considering the multiple learning styles and the impact of this apprenticeship in the child's life.

Investigating and understanding the different learning styles can help parents and educators in the development of the child's potential, as well as in the formulation of effective strategies for the student's learning, requiring the application of methods and techniques that accommodate the pedagogical needs of each learner.

Three different learning styles deserve attention in student's apprenticeship:

- Visual learners: learning is developed more easily when the student can visualize the information through images, images with words, pictures, engravings, graphics, abstracts in handouts and other materials where it's possible to learn visually. In order to get a better fixation of the studied content, these students can make use of text markers in the preparation of summaries of the read material. Another option is to make use of flash cards, where children can learn effectively memorizing the content displayed on each card.

- Kinesthetic learners: also known as tactile learners, these students better apprehend the knowledge when they can touch or feel when learning. As a teaching technique, the educator can apply activities in which the child can touch the materials and experiment with different textures and formats. In a class on geometric shapes, for example, instead of presenting texts and books on the subject, the teacher can show the class colored geometric shapes made of wood (or other material) that students can touch and feel using her or his fingers.

- Auditory learners: knowledge is better absorbed when the child has the opportunity to hear the content studied. This student can read texts or handouts in a loud voice as a learning strategy. The student can also be encouraged by the teacher to summarize, orally, what has been understood from the reading material. The use of jingles, poems and songs are auditory techniques that can enhance the child's learning as well as the utilization of lectures, discussions, debates, documentaries and audio tapes.

- Sometimes combining more than one of these strategies can also make a difference, for example combining visual and auditory, visual and kinesthetic, etc.

Different learning styles demand different ways of working with content and lessons, and this ends up making the learning process more dynamic. A child may have a dominant learning style or a blend of all of them. The important thing to know is that, to the extent that the child is stimulated, the more opportunities to develop and to appropriate other learning styles will be possible.

Promote learning environments that take into account the learning styles of each student; it is essential to provide a more effective and productive learning for the student. In a classroom where there are different learning styles (because each child is different from another one), you should cover all three learning styles, incorporating multiple techniques of teaching, in an attempt to promote an accessible knowledge for all the students. The following are some examples of how to incorporate the three learning styles in a learning environment:

- Visual learning style: the contents and the teaching techniques may include resources that the student can see and observe, such as maps, posters with examples or pictures on the subject studied in class, flip charts containing summaries of the notes made by the teacher with the help of the students, key words written by the child and highlighted with colored pen, typing of the words by the child and using highlighting features in Microsoft Office, use of flashcards for better fixation of the student's assignment or developing paper strips containing the main points on the revised lesson.

- Auditory learning style: children with auditory learning skills have facility to capture knowledge audibly and orally from the teacher's explanations in class such as through the exposure to a lecture or seminar on the subject of study or in discussions or debates with the classmates. These students also enjoy reading aloud the material that they are studying, as well enjoy recording audio parts of the material explained by the teacher in class.

- Kinesthetic learning style: the child's learning environment must include objects and spaces that he or she can touch, feel and experience. The educator can provide this student a variety of sizes, textures, shapes and materials such as paper, paint and graphite, geometric forms, experiments in the laboratory or outdoors, playing board games or in group dynamics, or theater plays about the content being studied.

When the teacher considers the learning style of each student, the knowledge is exposed in a perspicacious and effective way because the child is able to absorb the content according to what his or her senses better capture and process. In this way, the student develops, in an efficient and productive manner, the apprenticeships and skills needed for their individual learning.

When the school recognizes that there are different learning styles for each student, labels and unkind comments such as "lazy" or "disinterested" are discarded. The teacher has the opportunity to apply multiple methods and techniques of teaching, appreciating and considering the different ways of thinking and learning of the students.

The child in the classroom can also present other learning styles, manifested through multiple intelligences distributed in the human brain. The concept of multiple intelligences is the result of a study conducted by the American scientist Howard Gardner, who considers that the individual is able to learn and solve problems using a range of capacities and skills in:

- o Spatial intelligence: learning is most effective through the use of images and pictures;
- o Musical intelligence: the knowledge is best absorbed when there is the use of sounds and music during the learning;

- Linguistic intelligence: preference for using content in speech or writing in pedagogical activities;
- Kinesthetic intelligence: ability to use body movement to improve the knowledge of some content;
- Logical-mathematical intelligence: preference to use calculations and numerical data to solve problems and improve strategies of study;
- Interpersonal intelligence: facility to learn and study in groups. Ability to get along with the members of the class, managing to capture and administrate group ideas;
- Intrapersonal intelligence: in this style of learning, the student demonstrates ease and interest in working alone, using a strategy like self-study.

A person can manifest a particular dominant learning style or a mixture of them. There are also individuals who come to present different learning styles, according the different situations of apprenticeship that are experienced. What defines a person's learning style is the way his or her brain processes new information.

The human brain consists of two hemispheres: the right and the left hemisphere. The left hemisphere of the brain is responsible for functions involving logic, mathematics, planning and execution of activities. The right hemisphere is related to actions involving imagination and creativity as well as the capabilities of synthesis, rhetoric and language intonation.

The two hemispheres work in an integrated manner so that the person is able to develop daily tasks, making use of logic, creativity, thought, language, spatial organization, movement, among others, with the intent to contribute to the personal and academic development of the individual.

Regardless of the dominant style of learning that the child manifests, it is possible to develop other types of skills existing in human development, through the varied stimuli in the environment, at school and in the child's experiences.

19 TEACHING ADULT STUDENTS

Adult education involves teaching practices that are different from practices used with children. This is because an adult accumulates histories and life experiences that make him or her able to reflect and make decisions about his or her routine, knowledge and education. Thinking about it, Malcolm Knowles, an American specialist in adult education, denominated the learning process in the adulthood as "andragogy," that means "art or science to guide adults to learn." Andragogy is a term used to differentiate pedagogy, the education of children.

Learning gains value and significance for the adult when the object of knowledge involves the student's experiences and lifestyle practices. In this way, andragogy studies the best teaching practices oriented to the adult learner. The model based on andragogy consists of the following precepts:

1. The adult is motivated to learn what will make sense for his or her practice and for his or her life. Thus, new content must present a real significance and meaning to the adult student. It is necessary that the adult realizes that the new content will serve his or her daily routine and not remain only in books or handouts.

2. Each student learns in a particular way, according to his or her learning style. In this way, it is essential that the teacher understands the multiple styles of learning (visual, auditory and kinesthetic), in order to be able to understand that the knowledge is acquired and processed in a specific and different manner for each student.

3. The adult must have the opportunity to demonstrate what was comprehended and understood about the content learned. Adults learn by experience, so it is crucial that they can demonstrate and experience what they have learned. For example, these activities would be those in which they can discuss or debate, present practical examples of this new knowledge in their lives and perform tasks in groups where each student can expose his or her ideas and thoughts.

4. Children and adolescents have learning focused on themes, while the adult develops the apprenticeship oriented to problems. Adult students want to learn something that will help them in performing tasks and in the resolutions of problems.

5. It is necessary that adults have autonomy and freedom to learn, to realize that they are responsible for their own learning process, and be a protagonist in their education.

Teaching Reading And Writing To Adults With Special Needs

Special educational needs in adults are characterized by the difficulty in understanding, memorizing and learning some information and knowledge. This occurs because the brain collects and processes the information in a way that affects the comprehension and the development of the learning. The adult with special needs may have, for example, problems in reading, writing and performing math. So an adult that has difficulty with specific content can't be considered incapable or lazy. What happens is that the adult's brain receives and processes information being taught in a different manner.

Learning needs can affect both men and women, and it is estimated that the cause is related to some dysfunction in the central nervous system. The disorders can manifest in the routines of men and women throughout their lives, causing significant changes in behavior, emotions and learning.

It is worth emphasizing that issues such as lack of educational opportunities, absence of learning stimulus in childhood, or adaptation difficulties to the pedagogical method or to school, cannot develop a learning disorder in the student's life.

How To Identify In The Learning Environment, An Adult With Special Educational Needs

Special Needs in reading (Dyslexia): Dyslexia is a neurological disorder, which affects the reading, writing and comprehension of words, and this causes difficulty in how the student identifies the letters and the precise sounds of each word. The adult with dyslexia may also have difficulty in understanding the meaning of a few words, and in some cases, this student may exchange graphemes and phonemes in reading and writing sentences. Among the main features presented by the students are:

- Presence of difficulties in reading and writing
- Familiar historical problems in reading and writing
- Trouble in remembering names of people or places
- Confusion when pronouncing words with similar sounds
- Difficulty in reading sentences aloud
- While reading, the student replaces some words of the text by others that are non-existent
- Often pauses in words or parts of words while reading a sentence
- Hesitation or insecurity to use a few words during speech in the classroom or in the presence of many people
- Extreme fatigue during reading
- Preference for books or reading material with fewer words on a page and more pictures
- Constant need to reread sentences and texts in order to understand them better

- Requests the help of another person to read correspondence
- Difficulty in identifying and understanding the notions of right and left
- Develops handwriting containing capital letters with lowercase letters mixed
- Writes phrases and words in an abbreviated way
- Difficulty summarizing a text
- Spelling mistakes in the writing of texts and words

Types of dyslexia in Adults

Dyslexia has some subtypes containing specific characteristics such as:

- Dyseidetic Dyslexia or Visual Dyslexia: This type of dyslexia is characterized by a disorder in the eyes' visual processing that affects the ways it obtains information and sends it to the brain. In this type of dyslexia, the student has difficulties memorizing and remembering sequences of letters of the alphabet, letters to form a word, days of the week or months of the year. When the student needs to copy lessons and contents from the blackboard, it may present problems of visual discrimination and confusion of letters and similar words. The texts developed by the student may have different font sizes in the same sentence or reversals or omissions of letters both in reading and in writing.

- Dysphonetic Dyslexia or Auditory Dyslexia: In auditory dyslexia, the student has difficulty in associating phonemes with graphemes, often mistaking the sounds of words when pronouncing a phrase, especially with letters and words with similar sounds. Spelling can be a confusing task for a student with Dysphonetic Dyslexia because there is confusion in the discrimination of sounds and words.

- Mixed Dyslexia: in this type of dyslexia, the student can present characteristics of both types of dyslexia cited above.

There are also some types of dyslexia, which are identified according to the cause identified in the central nervous system, such as:

- Primary Dyslexia: This type of dyslexia is caused by inherited damage on the left side of the brain and does not change with increasing age.
- Secondary Dyslexia: can occur due to hormonal factors caused by poor nutrition of the fetus in the early stages of development. This type of dyslexia may decrease over time, more commonly appearing in boys than in girls.
- Trauma Dyslexia: can arise due to a brain injury or a serious injury to the head, in specific neural regions responsible for controlling the activities of reading and writing.

Students with dyslexia should have their eyes examined by a doctor, preferably a qualified professional who can diagnose Irlen syndrome, which along with dyslexia development, is a major cause of difficulty in reading and learning.

Irlen Syndrome

The Irlen Syndrome is a visuospatial disorder caused by the way the visual cortex of the brain processes information. This occurs because of a deficit in the central nervous system in encoding and decoding visual information. Therefore, it is considered a problem in visual perception and not a pathology related to the eye.

Identified in 1983 by the American psychologist Helen Irlen, the syndrome affects many aspects of life, especially activities involving reading and writing. Because it causes distortions in light waves, a person suffers high sensitivity to light and difficulty maintaining focus on reading activities.

In addition, students with Irlen Syndrome may have:

- Excessive tiredness due to the effort made while reading, presenting difficulties in sustaining reading tasks
- Difficulty in performing activities such as playing a ball or judging distances
- Discomfort when reading and seeing the letters of the words in books and magazines, due to distortions in graphic materials
- Headache, irritability, and dizziness
- Discomfort caused by reflections, fluorescent lights, bright lights (photosensitivity)
- Difficulty copying lessons from the blackboard
- Difficulty in typing and working on the computer

The application of colored overlays (acetate transparencies) on the texts or selective filters (colored lenses) helps individuals with learning difficulties; it improves the fluency of reading and attention, contributing to the student's academic abilities.

20 PROPOSED EDUCATIONAL STRATEGIES FOR WORKING WITH STUDENTS WITH DYSLEXIA AND READING DIFFICULTIES

Educational Kinesiology and Brain Gym

http://www.brighthubeducation.com/special-ed-learning-disorders/78479-educational-kinesiology-and-dyslexia/

Educational Kinesiology is a pedagogical approach that uses movement as a teaching strategy. The movements used are grouped under the title of Brain Gym, which are body movements that the student uses to develop and improve focus, concentration and attention to better the performance of his or her academic activities.

The Brain Gym was created by Dr. Paul Dennison in order to improve the learning of children with Attention Deficit Disorder and Dyslexia. Altogether, there are 26 movements of the Brain Gym that can be performed by children, youth and adults, with the aim to providing enhancements in the functioning of the brain.

In the specific cases of dyslexia, the Brain Gym seeks to work the right hemisphere and the left hemisphere of the brain through movement and development of sensory motor skills. Kinesiology enhances the learning in a ludic and dynamic way, promoting new competencies, ways of thinking and improvements in the writing and reading processes. Body movement promotes the development of new brain connections and helps students with dyslexia to cope with difficulties involving laterality, sequence, organization and concentration.

21 BRAIN GYM: EXERCISES

1. **Cross Crawl:** This exercise promotes the cooperation between the cerebral hemispheres from the alternation between arms and legs. In addition, it assists in capacities of attention, concentration and coordination of movements.

Cross Crawl

- It can be practiced standing or sitting. The right hand must cross and touch the left knee. The person lifts the knee and does the same thing with her or his left hand on her or his right knee, as if marching. He or she should perform this for 2-3 minutes.

2. **Brain Buttons:** This exercise helps to irrigate the brain, integrating the two cerebral hemispheres, through the concomitant movement of the eyes, aiding in capacities of attention and concentration of the visual system, assisting the student in reading and writing skills.

Brain Buttons

Brain Buttons

- Place the index finger and the thumb just below the collarbone, in effect, locating the brain buttons. With your other hand, locate the belly button.

  The student must massage the brain buttons at the same time as massaging the belly button. This should be done for 2 minutes.

  The exercise should be repeated using the other hand: the hand that that was on the belly button goes to cerebral button, and the hand that was on the cerebral button goes to the belly button.

3. **Hook-Ups:** This exercise is ideal for relieving stress, tension and anxiety, promoting well-being and tranquility to the student

because of the breathing movements and coordination of arms and legs.

Hook-Ups

- With the student sitting or standing, have him or her cross the right foot over his or her left foot (or vice versa). With arms extended forward, the student should join his or her palms and twist the right arm over the left, bringing the hands to the center of the chest. The same movement should be repeated with the interlaced left arm on the right.
The students should hold this pose for a few minutes, inhaling and exhaling.

The second part of the exercise is done with the legs uncrossed and flat on the floor. The student must join the fingertips to each other, forming a circle in the center of the body. With closed eyes, the student should inhale and exhale on a count 8 breaths.

Hook-Ups

- The second part of the exercise is done with the legs uncrossed and flat on the floor. The student must join the fingertips to each other, forming a circle in the center of the body. With closed eyes, the student should inhale and exhale on a count 8 breaths.

5. **The Elephant:** This exercise helps in visual perception, laterality, concentration, coordination and attention.

The Elephant

- The student supports the left ear on the left shoulder and then extends his or her left arm, moving it from side-to-side, up-and-down, as if making a semi-circle in the air. During the exercise, the student's eyes should follow the hand's movement. The activity should be repeated with the right side of the body.

4. **Lazy 8s:** This exercise promotes the integration of bilateral cerebral hemispheres, visuospatial abilities, positively assisting in reading and writing activities.

Lazy 8s

- The student draws the number eight or the infinity symbol in the air with her or his thumb. The student's eyes should move smoothly with the design, which should also be done with the thumb of the other hand.

5. **Thinking Cap:** This exercise helps in hearing, peripheral vision, attention, concentration and short-term memory.

Thinking Cap

Thinking Cap

- Sitting or standing, the student begins gently massaging the tip of the ear, unfolding gradually the curves that are part of it.

Thinking Cap

- The students should repeat the same thing on the other ear two more times.

Thinking Cap

- Finally, repeating the same movement on both ears simultaneously.

6. **Double Doodle:** The movements of this activity assist in motor coordination, laterality and in visuospatial abilities, providing improvements in reading and writing competencies.

Double Doodle

- The activity can be performed on a piece of paper or on the blackboard. The student will make a bilateral design using both hands simultaneously. For this, the student will have chalk or a pencil in each hand and will draw with either pencils or chalk, at the same time, on the sheet or board.

Double Doodle

Double Doodle

Double Doodle

7. **Energy Yawn:** These movements help to relax and relieve tension, providing benefits in the student's verbal communication, creativity, attention and concentration.

Energy Yawn

- When opening the mouth, the student must locate, with the fingertips, the muscle of the jaw on both sides of the face.

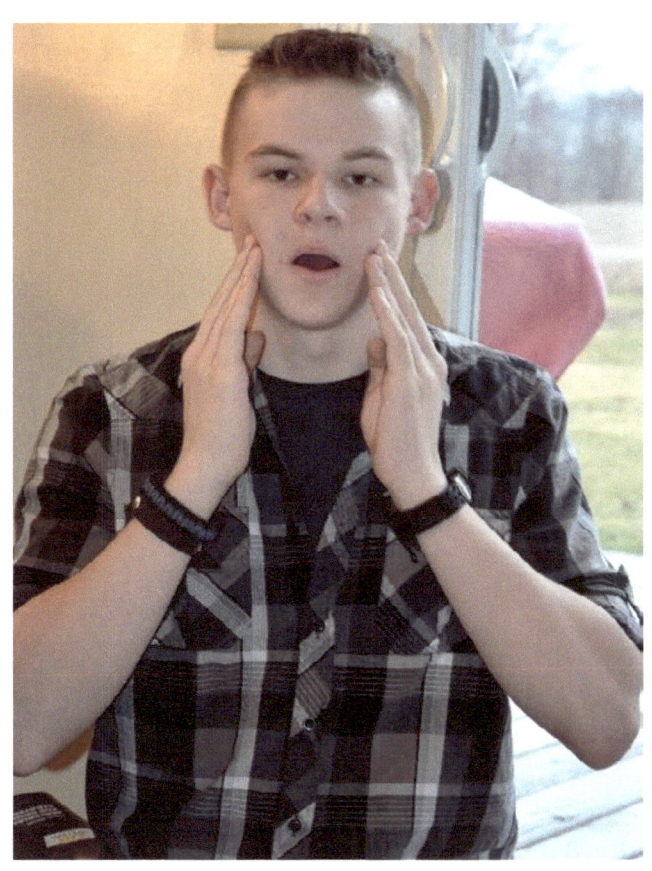

Energy Yawn

- After locating them, he or she should begin to massage the bones of the jaw gently, simultaneously developing small circular movements in the region on both sides of the face.

8. **Drink Water:** This practice contributes to the effectiveness of the central nervous system and the communication between neurons, in addition to promoting the balance between body and mind and, consequently, producing positive results for the student's development.

Drink Water

- Water is essential for good cerebral performance. Water contributes to better connectivity between the synapses (communication between neurons). Also, not drinking water causes loss of attention and concentration in a person because neural communication becomes impaired. Thus, the daily consumption of water is crucial to the effectiveness of the central nervous system. Drinking water throughout the day is essential for academic activities.

9. **Positive Points:** The movements of this exercise contribute to memory organization, concentration and emotional stability.

Positive Points

- With the fingers of each hand, the student locates a spot above each eye, between the hairline and eyebrows, and starts massaging these points smoothly and slowly. The student should close his or her eyes for better efficacy of relaxation and relief from stress.

Positive Points

Positive Points

10. **Arm Activation**: This exercise is indicated to be developed before, during, or after activities that involve computing and/or writing, because they relax the muscles, activate blood circulation and improve focus and concentration.

Arm Activation

Arm Activation

- This exercise can be done standing or sitting so that the arms can be free to move. The student should rise slowly, hold her or his arm in the air (at head height), and then must hold the elbow of arm raised, with the help of the other hand.

Arm Activation

- Finally, the arm extended should come down to the side of the body, slowly.

Arm Activation

- The same movement should be repeated with the other arm.

11. **Calf Pumps:** The movements of this exercise help in relaxation and contribute to a student's circulation and concentration. In addition, it brings benefits for interpersonal communication, improving expression and interaction skills.

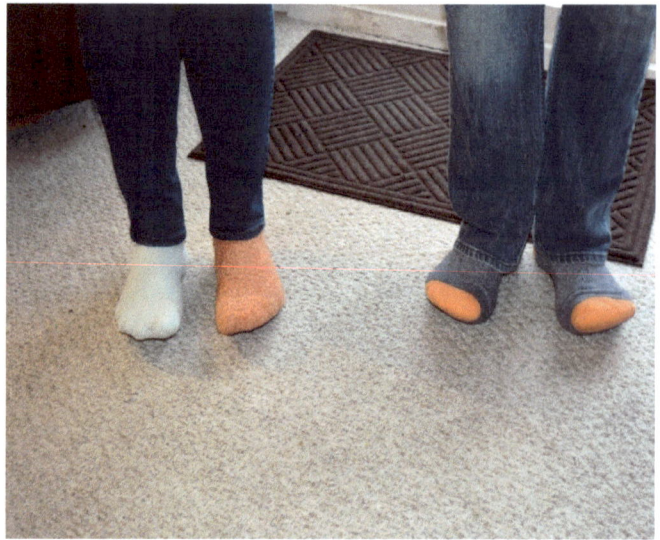

Calf Pumps

- With the student standing, he or she lifts his or her toes up and down, pulling the heel off the ground. The student should feel the stretch in the calf and only extend the toes as far as is comfortable. These movements can be made in a sequence of 3-5 times.

22 CONCLUSION

The purpose of the book *Unraveling Reading* is to encourage in students the love of learning to read and write by teaching it in a ludic and dynamic way.

The book presented a range of educational exercises and activities, as well as tips for encouraging children to read and develop writing skills.

It is important to remember that each student is unique and, therefore, has his or her own particular learning needs. In general, children learn best when the teacher mediates the lessons. While for the adult, the focus of learning is not so much in the teaching content but in the experiences that this student brings from their life.

The teaching method is a critical factor and can determine the progress or the difficulties a student might have in understanding what is being taught. Thinking about this, the author presented the three learning styles that can define the way that a student can comprehend the content in the classroom. There are three learning styles in the educational process: visual, kinesthetic and auditory style. Through practical activities involving the different learning styles in visual, kinesthetic, and auditory skills, the student will be able to absorb and process the lessons in a perspicacious and effective way.

Learning difficulties are a reality in the school context and understanding how learning is processed and absorbed by the human brain can be crucial for parents and educators who are developing and implementing activities according to the child's educational needs. Knowing how learning occurs in the brain is the key for educators to plan and implement more effective teaching techniques, so that the student can learn in the best possible manner. The brain, the organ by which information is processed, memorized and organized, and how to develop it better in favor of the learning, was a key theme in this book.

The application of exercises, which had as their objective the development of different parts of the brain involving multiple aspects of learning, especially on difficulties in reading and writing, were suggested as an effective strategy for students with special needs.

The Brain Gym exercises involve both cerebral hemispheres and aid in the learning process. The exercises increase the synaptic potential, strengthening the connections between neurons in the brain, promoting improvements in cognitive and motor skills and contributing to reading and writing lessons.

New Heights Educational Group hopes that this book can serve as a learning guide for parents, students and educators—promoting advances in the academic field and helping students overcome the difficulties involving learning to read and write.

23 DICTIONARY

Andragogy: is the science that studies the practice of teaching adults. The American educator, Malcolm Knowles, developed this theory in the 20th century, and according to him, adults are motivated by the experience and the need to associate what they learn with situations of everyday life. In addition, adults need to know why it is important to learn certain content or a lesson, in order to verify whether the knowledge taught in the classroom, will be of value to their lives.

Bibliographic: It is a term used to determine the names of research sources of a book, an academic project, a magazine, newspaper or article. The purpose of a bibliography is to document the work, reporting to readers the source of published material.

The bibliographic reference of a book, for example, must contain the last name and the author's name, book title, place of publication, publisher, and year. For example:

Stout, Kathryn. Natural Speller. USA: Study Design-A-1997.

Educational Kinesiology: supports learning through movement. The concept was developed by the learning specialist, Dr. Paul E. Dennison, and brings together a set of exercises termed Brain Gym. The exercises have techniques that integrate the two cerebral hemispheres, through movements that aim to develop the skills of reading, writing, calculation, communication, coordination, concentration and memorization. In addition, the activities contribute to controlling breathing and stress relief, balancing emotions and recovering self-esteem.

Flashcards: The flashcard is a set of cards (which may be made of paper or cardboard) and each contains a question on one side, and a response from the opposite side. The activity with flashcards consists of asking questions in order to get the largest possible number of correct answers on the subject being studied.

Example: if the student is studying a vocabulary list, the teacher can write on one side of the card a word, and in the opposite side the meaning of this word.

Graphemes: is a letter or a number of letters, which represent sounds, when a word is spelled. For example, the word 'ghost' contains five letters and four graphemes ('gh,' 'o,' 's,' and 't').

Laubach Learning System: It is a literature, focused on adult education published by New Readers Press. The Laubach method was elaborated to help adults with limited or no reading skills to develop competences in reading and writing.

Ludic: it refers to recreational practices that aim to entertain and amuse people. The concept of ludic activity in education involves body movements and playful activities in order to develop learning competences, such as reading and writing, with games, group dynamics, music, outdoor exercises, among other movements with the body.

Orthographic: It refers to a set of grammar rules that serve to guide the correct way to write a word or a text, respecting the signs of accentuation and punctuation.

Pedagogy: is the science that studies the practice of teaching children. The pedagogy involves understanding principles, methods and strategies to better develop the child's apprenticeship. This science is concerned with the process of teaching and learning in the classroom, seeking first to understand the needs and difficulties of the child, in order to apply appropriate techniques and contents, which can stimulate child's abilities.

Perspicacious: characteristic of a person who has the ability to understand content and information more easily than others can. It concerns the student who has excessive perception to understand things in a fast, easy way.

Phonemes: Phoneme is the smallest sound element able to establish a distinction of meaning between words, through the sounds of spoken language. Example: for 'Mommy.' The 'm' sound, / m /, is an example of a phoneme.

www.ingramcontent.com/pod-product-compliance
Lightning Source LLC
Chambersburg PA
CBHW041802160426
43191CB00001B/10